AVOCADO THOUGHTS

Printed in the United States of America

Book Baby Publishing in conjunction with
AVOT Avocado Thoughts LLC

Epilogue

You're always one choice away from a
completely different trajectory.
There's no avoiding the human experience.
When we believe we're taking "the easy route", it can quickly
lead to more unnecessary bumps in the road (whilst still being
purposeful). The more we think we know, the more we begin to
realize we know nothing at all.
Gratefully humbled by this ever-wavering experience.

Eternal gratitude to my massive support system. My family &
soul community have held me down; it's only law that I go UP.
If not for others, my love would be meaningless.

Let there be innocence.
Let there be freedom.
Let there be creativity
recharged by the sun.
Precious reminders that we too are a part of nature.

Dear soul, I'm still
learning about what
you love. I'm going
to give us more of
that; I promise.

Chapter 1

Word to my Body: I promise to never abandon my breath.

You better start acting like abundance is your birthright. You deserve everything you want in this lifetime. Start putting the work in & watch it all happen for you.
Be selective in what you focus on & what you spend time thinking about. Keep practicing & listening to your inner voice. Keep people close who are supportive & have genuine intentions.
Discipline will get you further than motivation.

Abandoned

There's comfortability in abandonment.
Loneliness finds its way around,
Creeping in the dark like I didn't leave it there,
As if I wasn't the one to keep me there.
Abandoned!
Is this what loneliness feels like?
Can you see me?
Can you see what abandonment looks like?
Codependency is like a drug – feening for a plug.
When will choosing me be easy?
Or is it easier to lose me?
Abandoned!
Like I don't know what it's like to be found,
Or if I'll ever be worth you staying around.
I pray to God out loud.
Can you hear me?
Can you hear what abandonment looks like?
Imperfection meets my projections.
Asking, is this all I'll ever be?
Abandoned!

Acceptance of Faith

Every day that it rained,
It led me to believe that the sun was nonexistent.
That the God I've been praying to was maybe nonexistent too.
Like I couldn't be heard, or even seen at one point.
I tried to hold space for fate and trust because I needed to believe
in something greater than myself.
I would say it doesn't hurt me to have faith but then again,
I'd be pretending.
Like walking away from everything I knew didn't leave me black and blue.
As if these scars of mine don't tell stories about centuries of pain.
Like the women in my family before me weren't
forced to not have a voice of their own.
Maybe they too were owned by their own demons.

So today,
I free them.
I free them from the trauma.
Today, I rewrite my story.
Not only for me but for all the women before me.
And for all the little girls with dreams bigger than their hearts.
It's time for a new start.
It's time we have faith.
Leaning into the acceptance of faith.
Spreading it across this world like water.
It's time we have faith
that something greater than us is working FOR us.
May we find the courage to STRATEGIZE & SCRUTINIZE
the blueprints our ancestors left for us.

To all the missing girls,
May you discover the courage
to find your way home.
A place of security, without worry.
A home filled with words that hold you despite
the reality that shrinks you.
You are beauty deeper than your skin.
You are magic, not an optical illusion.
I can see you.
I can feel you.
I know you and honor you.
Exactly-the way you are;
come home missing girl.

You vs You

Many identities stem from the
comparison of the others.
No more stories.
No more feeling like you need to be everything all at once.
No more feeling the need to escape through "ascension".
No more comparison-based realities.
No more shape-shifting to feel safe.
No more living in fight or flight.
No more pretending out of fear of abandonment.
Only trust.
In every moment.
It's less about "finding" who we are & more about getting out of the way,
so who we've always been can exist in balance.
Judging the external is a scape goat for non-self-acceptance.
It's safe to live without comparison.
It's nearly impossible to co-create a new
story or reality while holding onto old beliefs.
let go of what no longer serves you.
Don't let your mind be caught in a loop perpetuated by fear.
Keeping us safe while also keeping our dreams at bay.
I'm not here to tell you what is or isn't serving you.
You already know, regardless if the mind has awareness of it or not.
You KNOW because you FEEL it.
This is an invitation to FEEL for your beliefs.
Shift them so they are empowering you entirely.
I'm qualified to lead myself because I am devoted to constant self-love, transformation
and experience.

You are loved.

You are so loved.
I hope to only love you more,
listen more,
gravitate towards getting right.
Forgive more,
dream more.
More fearlessness versus comfortability.
More joy versus happiness.
More listening.
More loving.
More of we.
More of Us.
More Life.

If the people we attract in our lives are a direct reflection of where we are at with ourselves, when triggered by mistreatment or disrespect, ask yourself, "why do I treat myself this way?"

There is a difference between holding space for someone and allowing them to walk all over you by giving away your power. When you no longer feel the need to react or meet certain people where they are, you can meet yourself where you need to be. With kindness. With love.

Self-love

There is no loving others
without loving yourself.
Others are just a
projection of you.
The world is just a projection
of your inner self.
How do you expect to receive love
& acceptance if you can't
provide that for yourself?
One thing that is
helping on this
continuous journey of
self-love is knowing my
love language & showing
it to myself.
Continue to show gratitude to the
blessings in your life.

Purple Umbrella

What it means to INNERstand.
To INNERstand is to hold space while remaining under your own umbrella of experiences.
To stand in YOUR truth.
It isn't helpful
to understand or trauma bond.
When we INNERstand, we have
a deeper resonance with ourselves which allows us to be there for others.
You do not have to understand someone to show compassion
& Empathy.
Nor to truly understand someone, do you have to experience their pain.

Or

be willing to feel their pain.
We are emotional beings with an
incredible capacity to love.
That love can quickly turn to sludge
when we trauma bond.
When we attach our trauma to others, we give away the responsibility we have with ourselves to transmute
this trauma.

Causing codependency and
an unhealthy attachment.
You do not have to stand under anyone else's umbrella.
We are powerful enough to solely swim our way to emotional freedom.
We are all deserving of support.
Sometimes we need a push, a hug, a thoughtful gesture, kind words & energetic support but we do NOT need anyone else under our umbrella.
An umbrella is typically only effective when one person is under it, otherwise, someone gets wet.

Footnote: A trauma bond is a relationship or dynamic that plays out between two or more people who have endured similar trauma.

Abundance

Time spent waiting.
Waiting for someone to tell me that my gifts are brilliant
&
deserve to be shared with the world.
Waiting for someone to give me permission to flow
outside of
the box.
Waiting for someone to push me past my limiting beliefs
that I
only hold on to out of habit.
Waiting for someone to tell me aligned action is not
exclusive.
Waiting for someone to show up even though I wasn't.
All the excuses & reasons WHY not
were never outside of me
and never will be.
I am here right now because of me.
Just as guides, support & tools will only get us
so far, we must CHOOSE to jump with faith or
be waiting for a savior forever.
I believe in you.
Remembering how to believe in myself
FULLY,
Finding the unwavering abundance of
aligning with my truth.
To the unfolding of love
where time ceases to exist.
In the midst of becoming undecided
Folding in and out
Where time has no limits.
For the possibilities of becoming
Are endless.
The only way to fully receive is to
surrender.
Abundance is actualized through Trust.

"Projection makes perception"

We look inside first, decide the kind of world we want to see
and then project that world outside, making it the truth as we see it.
Realizing that our negative self-beliefs
are nothing more than stories is not disassociation;
it's detaching from the idea that you are your behaviors.
How do we expect to evolve while holding
onto a character we made up?
One experience from the Eternal Infinite of Life and the Mind
decides to become certain and carry that certainty into new experiences.
Jaded.
Until we choose to shift perspective.
Until we're willing to feel how powerful we truly are.
Until we see that our capacity to hold Love is beyond human measurement.
Acceptance.
Surrender.
Grace.
You are not your last behavior.
No matter how many times you have "messed up" doing the
"Same thing again & again"
You are not your last behavior.
At your core, you are innocent love.

An
embodied
woman
doesn't
worry about
what other
grown
women are
doing or
how they
look.
In a world full
of anxiety &
shallow
breathing,
take
a deep breath
and focus on your embodiment.

Sometimes people's "expectations" of you
are simply a reflection of the work they have failed to do for themselves
or where their needs weren't met by others.
You owe it to yourself to not take this personal.
They'll never be satisfied anyway.
So live for YOU every day.

When Manifesting:

1. Always stay positive and have gratitude.
2. Say it like it has already been accomplished.
3. Do not spend energy thinking about the adverse to what you desire.
4. Meditate and think often about what you want.
5. See it, feel it, hear it, believe it.
6. Decide that it's real in your brain, therefore, it will be real in the physical.
7. Lastly, be specific as to what you desire.

"Everything is working out for me no matter how it looks at any point in time".

With realization, comes hard promise:

There is someone out there who will make certain
you know their intentions and feelings.
It will exclaim in every fiber of their being.
You won't have to justify their actions because
they will already read true and genuine.
You won't have to settle for common interactions
because the majority of their actions will be wrapped in
love and thoughtfulness.
As much as it hurts not to be chosen,
Rest assured:
You have already been chosen by you
and you are all you need.
You know your desires and what you bring to the table.
Someone will wake up and choose you every day because
they want to build with you.
If you feel you must prove,
in action or description,
that you should be chosen,
you are doing yourself a disservice.
So, wait.
Wait for the genuine love that can happen and grow
organically.
Wait for that person who will wake up and choose you
every time no matter the circumstance.
Who will love and choose you at your best and your
worst.
Most importantly,
choose yourself every day,
over and over again.

Detachment = Disassociation

Passenger consciousness is fully embracing the experience
presenting itself while simultaneously detaching from everything other
than your responsibility.
The only way to truly know the difference
is to discern with complete & utter honesty with yourself.
Detachment is NOT avoidance.
Detachment IS trusting.
Detachment is NOT escapism.
Detachment IS acceptance.
The key is to not skip steps and bypass.
Honor the reality happening through you
without identifying it as absolute.
Everything is temporary.
Everything is perfect.
Your response is the frequency.
Your frequency creates the biofeedback.
Either we're co-creating timelines or getting caught in time loops.
The choice is always ours.
Sometimes
We have to play in the loops until we're ready to jump timelines.

Honor Where You Are At With Transparency & Meet Yourself With Grace

Stressing about a self-created timeline can lead to unwise decisions.
Settle your spirit.
You didn't miss it.
What is for you is still unfolding.
Be in love with being alive.
Find passion in life itself.
Be addicted to being a better version of yourself every day
Know that you can always start over if you're not proud of the life you're living.

Direction is so much more important than speed.
Some are going nowhere, fast.
Follow the path that leads from your heart.
That path will lead you on the uncharted journey called life.
And when it does,
Everything will happen for you suddenly and you'll be thankful you didn't give up.
Blessings are coming.
Believe that and keep working.
Embrace the adversity and you will be better because of it.

When people don’t know their purpose,
They hate you for living yours.
Do not let this world make you calloused.
Continue to give as you are able to.
You should give from a cup that overflows
Rather than needing to be poured.

They were a part of me.
We both didn't understand how to accept love.
They were raised on survival, and I was raised on love.
That alone was not enough to save us.
It got to the point where we pushed everyone away.
Including each other.

Timing is critical.
Yet,
we let time pass endlessly every day
Right person, wrong time.
All in the plan above.
It's not my plan in fact.
We rush.
We plan.
we get so upset when things don't work out how we want them to.

Sound Affirmations.
Right person.
Right time.

Trust

It can be lost; it can be gained.
Once you lose it,
it can be hard to attain it once more.
There are times when you lose it
and it reflects on the nothingness that is owed to you.
I trust you means that I am giving you every unwavering benefit of doubt
until you give me a reason not to.
I am beginning to remember what it's like to trust again.
Like I never forgot.
As if I've always known.
Yet never known.
Water remembers.
Water holds the want for emotional sovereignty.
It's safe to remember that we never forgot.
It's safe to trust her.
It's safe to trust you.
I am home.
I am safe.

Before it All

I appreciate you.
I understand that you are in a different headspace
and that some of your thoughts are from a different perspective.
I enjoy our friendship.
I love this the most.
I care about you and where you want to be.
I enjoy spending time with you
because time with you is well spent.
Your happiness makes me happy, and that is so lovely.
Unconditionally,
I appreciate you and understand your struggles.
I appreciate your struggles because your struggles are what shape you.
I appreciate where you are at in life.
I care about you
and
I care about where you end up.
The type of love I have for you is different from the love I have for myself.
I owe that to me.
When you know better, you do better.
In order to love you,
I need to love me.
I'm doing better, loving me.

TRUSTING

I am protected and guided with each breath.
I have everything I need with me.
When I am fearful,
I love myself.
I trust and love myself for there is nothing to fear.
Today & every day, I practice TRUSTING.
Fear is cultivated in the mind,
then taken on by the body.
Where the mind goes,
the body follows.
Fear is an illusion.
I choose to replace fear with faith.
When worry or uncertainty becomes present,
I choose to trust.

Where you find comfort outside of yourself
will soon become a reflection of what you are unwilling to give to yourself first.
For that which you seek must be made clear.
Be honest with yourself.
You don't do yourself any favors if you aren't 100% honest with yourself
about how things are going and how you are behaving.
Notice behavior patterns.
We are all creatures of habit.
Some of these habits are helpful and others are not.
It's good to be aware of your habits so you can actively weaken the ones you don't want and strengthen the ones you do want.
Be able to articulate your core values.
If you don't know what's important to you,
how can you ever grow and manifest your best self?
Take time to consider what's most important to you so that you can better evaluate whether you're living those values.
Be forgiving.
Change is hard and old habits are hard to break.
Be gentle with yourself when you don't get it right.
It's okay.
We're all human.
We all make mistakes.
Keep track of you.
Pour into you at your lowest and at your prime.

Gratitude

Let's practice praying
when we have all that we need,
not just when we're desperate for what we desire.
Flow & let go.

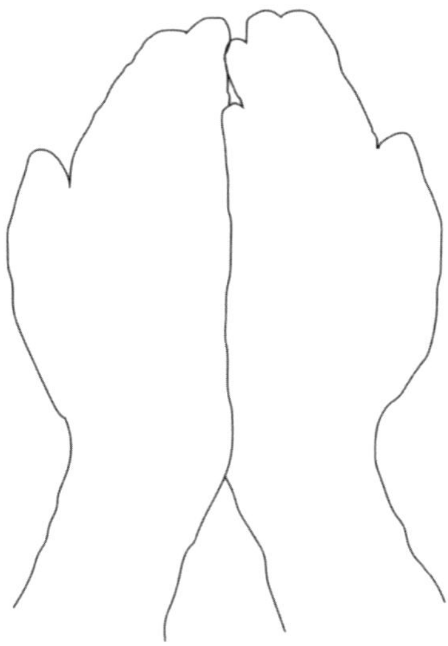

Puzzle Pieces

The pieces are everywhere.
You may not be able to see
the bigger picture
or see it clear.
The picture is me.
One by one,
Day by day,
I am the one who pieces this puzzle together.
I am the one solving the puzzle.
I am the puzzle.
The puzzle is me.

Change

I didn't change for you.
I changed upon experiences.
I changed for me,
to become a better me.
I changed to heal myself first.
Emotional detachment is my disassociation.
I am creating emotional awareness through my feelings.
My emotions are trapped within my body.
I am recognizing when they are influenced or triggered.
Observing this energy in motion as it moves through my body,
I am creating a safe place within to feel without judgement blame or shame.
I am transmuting my energy to those who are deserving by expressing gratitude.
For these are the guides that observe my external reality without the emotional body making it too personal.
You may not be able to see the path that I am on and that is okay;
it's not your path.
But don't expect someone to stay if you are never there.

You won't get in the way of my dreams
because
you are part of my wildest dream.

Remind yourself of the bigger picture.
If you want to fly,
you must give up the stuff that weighs you down.
You can rise from anything.
You can completely recreate yourself.
Remember, nothing is permanent.
You are not stuck.
You have choices.
You can think new thoughts and surround yourself with new people.
You can learn new things and create new habits.
What matters is that you decide today and never look back.
Are we actually willing to invest in ourselves by letting go of the things
that no longer serve us
or
are we
only interested in holding onto the
story of why we never could
Let go
And
just dream.

SAFE

I love feeling safe enough to be the
soft version of me.
I don't want to
constantly be on defense.
I operate best when I'm moving in
delicacy
and
love.
I am clear:
I am relaxed.
I am at peace.
I am open.
I am.
As I begin to breathe deep into my belly, all tension
releases.
I am safe.

We always have a choice.
Daily reminder that
the projection field is
like a fun house & I
know who I am by
releasing who I'm NOT
with EASE & GRACE.

MIND YOUR OWN

Minding your business is a rhetoric used to
remind others that when you focus on yourself,
you have a lot more time to take care of yourself.
What I consume in entirety
is my CHOICE.

It's each person's choice to choose what they feel is right for them
RIGHTFULLY.
So my body does not concern you.
Your body does not concern me.
I trust that my body
is equipped to handle anything.
She is strong.
If you don't feel that way about your body,
that is YOUR responsibility
to do what feels right for you
and I
respect that.
I can't help you.
You can't help me.
Nobody
outside of us can save us unless we make a choice for ourselves.
In reality, the best thing you can do for someone else
is *TAKE CARE OF YOURSELF.*
As a collective,
we've been programmed to desire instant gratification to escape our own choices.
I co-create with my EVERYDAY choices.
Not for a sticker.
Not for adrenaline or a dopamine rush.
Not to fit in.
Not to prove a point.
Not to follow the herd.
Not out of fear &
Absolutely NOT because someone told me to.
I am FREE.
You are FREE.
We are FREE.

Together

We were both in the process of liberating ourselves
From dynamics that no longer served Us.
Remembering what it was like to be whole within
ourselves as individuals.
We held so much unconditional space for each other as
friends,
a catalyst for our growth.
We're so similar, yet so different & I honor that about Us.
Communication.
Trust.
& Respect
is the backbone
of how we walk
in this Life.

TRUTH

How long will you fight off who you are to keep who you aren't alive?
Here in lies the truth of all truths.
Where every truth is true,
separation ceases to exist
within the flow of every breath,
the wind sweeps in to remind us
how light we truly are.
how bright we truly are.
As the sun climbs the clouds,
she emanates the gift of life;
a rise each day.
The fall at the sight of the stars.
The simplicity in being is so transparent, yet the veil drapes the same.
As I let go with each breath,
a newer version of self emerges.
The self that has always been dormant,
volatile in expression because
lightning strikes before the sound of thunder.
Still, I allow softness in.
I submerge in it.
It's safe to swim home.

How Many of Us Have Them?

Friends don't count favors.
Let them show you their true colors.
You are not my friend.
You are a distraction.

Roses

You're supposed to clip the roses my dear...
Trim the leaves,
cut the ones with no life
so that the nutrients can be absorbed by the whole plant.
Keeping dead leaves blocks the nutrients from the plant.
You are just watering old habits and dead situations.
Stop blocking your blessings.

CHAPTER 2:

Happiness
the love I have for myself.
Soul full of sunshine.
Drink your water and mind your own.
We ain't got time for all that other stuff.

Be an uncynical believer.
Believe that good things happen to good people.
Believe that good things will happen,
and they will.
Believe that they will,
and they will.

A BLACK QUEEN

I find comfort in my solitude.
I am alone, but I am not lonely.

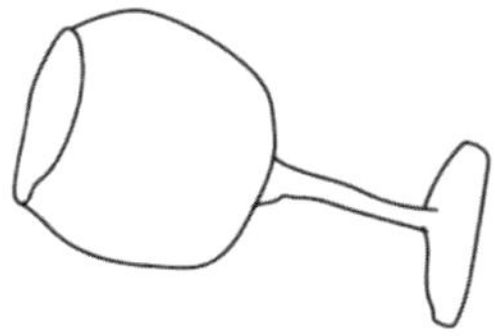

I used to
be so
hung up
on trying to fix everything.
Trying to save every relationship
friends or not.
Overpouring,
Draining,
Empty was my glass.
Life goes on
with or without.
Taking time to refill
Me & Mines.
Focus on you and yours,
others will fall into place
or get out of the way.
Life goes on.

You are my safe haven and
greatest guide to conquering my challenges.
You are my unshakable rock and
the greatest whirlwind of a human.
You are strong in your values and
the greatest reminder to not take life too seriously.
You are my loyal best friend
and greatest love.
You are my greatest everything
I love you,
my love.

Ten-Fold

Maybe you've been given this time
to remind yourself of who you really
are and what you need out of life.
Stop comparing and just appreciate your process and journey.
Your struggles and your story are meant to inspire a totally different group of people.
Don't complain, but
understand
that this is your story
and it will be special
if you don't fold.

Her

When you take the time
to learn who you are
& learn how to control your mind,
That's when true happiness sets in.
When life doesn't happen to you,
It starts happening FOR you.
That's living.
Self-love is a daily practice,
not an overnight celebrity.
A dedication to oneself,
An honoring in every now moment.
My truth is,
I have fallen away from this.
I have allowed the subconscious programming to decide
for me
a reminder that
you are never too far from self to love again & again &
again.
I am still
learning to love my body every day.
She needs me and I need her.

Wholeness

May the stories of who you believe you are
dissolve into the truth of your true essence.
You are not the idea of yourself.
Be at peace with this.
Knowing a thought that creates beliefs
are Reality Shapeshifters.
I am safe to create.
I am innocence.
I am whole.
I am purity.
I am.
I trust in the Divine within me.

With Compassion & Grace,
You'll be surprised
What happens when you allow yourself
to get curious about what the body is capable of.
Get to the other side of overcoming;
It is such a rewarding feeling.
You won't know until you tap in
it's better over here.

Oneness is a collective of Individuality.
I release the need to overextend.
I release the need to over-explain.
I release the need to match frequency.
I release the need to leave the now.
I release what no longer serves me.
"My need to "do" transforms into my desire to be"

You can write
“I am worthy"
in a journal
Or
say it aloud to yourself daily.
Nothing will shift
Until
your belief shifts
which means the old agreement
has transfigured into something else.
Words cast spells because of the meaning
we give them.
Words are just words until
they are powered by our belief.
Words are spellbinding.

Talking about others
eventually gets old
because you realize your
subconscious mind
has really been
talking
about itself.

Perception is subjective,
somewhat collective,
then again, reality lies within
the eyes of the beholder.
A hands-on kind of learner
to only be able to learn through self-experience,
never feeling quite normal
and always borderline too far left,
really just in her own world.
Extending her love way too much
emotional and overly sensitive,
she sees the world through her heart
not through her eyes.

Liberator.
I am human.
Imperfection is contrast.
Contrast is humbling.
I manifest from within.
I am deserving.
I am the physical manifestation
of abundance.
I am abundance
when I believe in myself.
I create space for others to do the same.
My family was brought from over-seas.
We did what we could with what we had
and through their generations,
there is liberation.

Pintor

You are the artist & the paint brush.
Within every given moment
is an opportunity to pivot,
Expand
& transform.
There are no boundaries,
for they have been
created by you,
for you &
through you.
You are the bounds & the bountiful.
Fly high baby bird
for there are no limits.

Forgiveness & Compassion
is the compass out of Regret.
Forgiving myself
for not seeing my innate worth organically.
My thoughts create my reality.
My words create my reality.
My body language creates my reality.
My breath creates my reality.
My conscious choice creates my reality.

Continued

I choose to create from my heart because
I am worthy.

Release + Reassess + Reconfigure.

Send Me Into Orbit

I love reflecting through photos
currently navigating timelines of uncharted territory
as I shed the many layers of She.
One foot in,
one foot out.
"Is it safe to step out,
to step into this new embodiment?"
Slow & steady
Meeting myself where I'm at.
The in-between phase is where the magic happens.
I welcome my heart to express itself as the rainbow bridge between worlds.
This is your invitation to allow grace into your heart.
Meet yourself where you're at,
even if that may appear as light years away from your desired destination.
You are everything
you desire in this NOW moment.
You are whole & complete,
always,
in all ways.

To the hair on my legs,
the bruises on my shins,
the scars,
stretch marks
engrained on my temple,
I love you.
Your body needs
YOUR touch.
YOUR love.
Let me help you help yourself.
Let me love you.
Let me show you how to love the most awkward
Insecure
Parts of you.
That is love.
This is love.
This is you.

Home

The unhappiness you feel now
leads to overthinking.
Overthinking stresses you out.
There are more tears today than in all the days before you.
I want you to be happy
but I cannot do that for you.
Happy for you is a destination.
In reality,
happy is now.
Happy is here.
Happy is home.
I get to be here now.
I choose to be here now.
I am here now.
I am home.
I am happy.

Distance means so little
when someone means so much.
Your Happiness makes me happy and that is so lovely.
Happy to be here with you.
Happy to love you.
Love is helping even when you don't know how.
Love is holding you and the tears when you don't want to be held.
Love is helping yourself.
My love is too much to be thrown back in my face.
At the same time,
you can't expect anyone else
to take care of your problems.

CHAPTER 3

We mismanage time because we are scheduling the result instead of the process.
Where I am today is where I need to be tomorrow.

When you carve out a niche
and grind for years to develop a unique lucrative skillset,
you are valuable.
If those around you do not see this,
find new people.
Spend as little time as possible convincing people of your worth.
The depth of your pain
is an indication of the height of your growth.
If you're going through a transition,
keep going
because at the end is joy
Success
Happiness
Peace.
Let your results speak for themselves.
Survive.

Midnight Thoughts 3.12.21

I don't have it all together.
Oftentimes I feel like I'm always falling apart
starting over.
Feeling like abstract art....
beautifully confusing
searching for myself
high and low.
Maybe this is how I grow
Being forced to let go
of who I once was.
Scared
because metamorphosis is a painful transition.
Desperate to break through.
To become new.
To become "she who grew".

I was never too hard to love.
You just didn't know how-
to love yourself.
I extended my hand to you
For you to pull me down with you.
How could I save me
when I couldn't save you?
I was never meant to.
We were never meant to.
You were the one hard to love.
The one I could never get to.

- Grateful
- to have reached me.

Hurricane

Do you have to witness a hurricane to know the ocean is real?
The eye of a hurricane is said to be the calmest part of the storm.
Therefore,
I choose to stand in the center of it all.
I don't have to be physically near or far.
I simply am.
I do not fear the storm because I become the eye,
not destructive,
powerful.
Embracing and accepting with arms wide open
isn't always a walk in the park,
But it is a dance into the arms of compassion.
My reflections have been guiding me deeper into compassion
for others and more deeply
for myself.
The more I accept
I am the storm,
the less resistance
I create with the world around me.

Patience is pleasure
because you're worth the wait.
- slow down;
vital energy
sexual energy
life force energy.
When we allow ourselves to slow down and enjoy each moment,
every breath is as purposeful as the last.
There is pleasure in intention;
That's why it feels so good to accomplish a goal
rather than the attainment of that goal itself.
The reflection we paint in society is that of destination.
An outside dream painted by the projections
of the unknown filtered but the subconscious,
the process,
the steps in between
the smallest,
tiniest pieces
make up the whole fractals
appearing as separate.
Pleasure is found in the depths of patience
bearing the most succulent fruit.
You are worth the wait
because
time is an illusion.
You are in every moment,
whole.
There's no "time" to rush.

Gratitude

I live in a state of gratitude.
We receive in gratitude.
I always receive exactly what I ask for
& I appreciate that.
I am eternally grateful for the love I am capable of giving
& for the love I have yet to receive.
I am grateful now
& that
is keeping the
door open for more blessings.
And so it shall be.

I am fully equipped to care for my own vessel.
My senses catapult me into infinite growth.
I am innocence.
I am safe to express myself.
I am pure energy.
I am sensual and creative.
I respect myself.
I am intentional.
I am aware.
I am expressive.
I am intuitive.
I am unique.
I am.
When my heart sings,
Love returns.
I am secure in my body.
I am honored in my body.
I am seen in my body.
I am felt in my body.
I am heard in my body.
I am.

Discipline is a virtue.
It must be watered daily to grow.
There's this idea that discipline is restriction.
Being disciplined is "strict".
Discipline is Honor.
Choosing to be our own parent
and deciding what's best for us in this now moment is liberation.
If we haven't been watering ourselves in this practice, restriction or resistance appears when the ego is simply the observer.
We complicate what's innately simple,
so it's overlooked.
Inner guidance is overlooked
because it sways away from the destruction awaiting to rebirth you.
Willpower & Accountability are not chores but CHOICES.
Free yourself from the idea that structure means control.
Amidst distractions & projections,
there is always a choice.
Our inner child always has a choice
but is not the deciding factor.
Am I choosing in the now moment
Or
is my emotional body choosing for me
based on past traumas + experiences?
Ask yourself.

I am open to new adventures.
I am open to receive.
I am confident.
I am wondrous.
I am.
It is my brightness to experience life in bliss.
The efforts you make to heal
and grow are seen by the universe.
Become more aware
of what is really worth
your energy.
Trust me,
you inspire people who pretend to not even see you.

I am a force of light.
I am a source of love.
I am grounded by my roots.
I am eternal youth.
I am.
I invite joy and playfulness with each breath.
I call back my energy.
I call back my power.
I call back my projections.
I call back any energy leaks.
When I call back my waters,
liberation is birthed.

You resonate with the energy you receive.
Surround yourself with high vibrations
and magic will happen.

I am

Divine intelligence works through me with each breath.
I am grateful for my breath.
I am grateful for love.
I am grateful for community.
I am grateful for divine reflections.
I am grateful as I am.
I am infinite gratitude.
I am.
Deep reverence fills my being as each breath
tends to my internal waters.
I am divinely connected to my vessel.
I am the energy that powers my physical body.
I am open to receive divine guidance.
I am endless wisdom.
I am.
I am not my vessel.
I am more than my body.
I am.

My reflection was never enough & hiding was one of
my greatest talents. I was still outsourcing and giving my
power away, but I continued to say yes to myself in the
ways I knew how.
Conscious relationships are not "problem-free".
They require deep devotion & honor.
Love is a choice.
I choose you always
& you have shown me to choose myself.

Today's Daily Affirmations:
March 12, 2018

I am wealthy in abundance.
Abundance loves me.
I am deserving of wealth.
Everything I desire is making its way to me.
Everything is working out for me no matter how it looks at any point in time.

Who is at the door?

I keep the long-term goals in the back of my head.
They tend to be a distraction for the short-term ones.
-Anxiety

You are blessed and fearless.
If you stick to your principles,
things will work out.
Take the leap
Now, this right here,
this is the move.

Fail Forward

I know I've failed.
I've failed many times.
But failure is a part of the process.
Fail forward and trust the process.
Keep Failing.
Failure is like gravity; what goes up will eventually come down.
Success is coming;
be patient.

A Plate of Veggie Dumplings

Savory
Sweet
Plump
Goodness
Full
I am
Full of Life
Full of goodness
Living a Full Life.
Adventurous
Outside my comfort zone.
Outside of my palate
Outside of my everyday plate
Every Friday.
She comes and
goes.
Today is the day.
I have asked the
lady on the
Harlem corner
to try a bowl of
her veggie
dumplings.

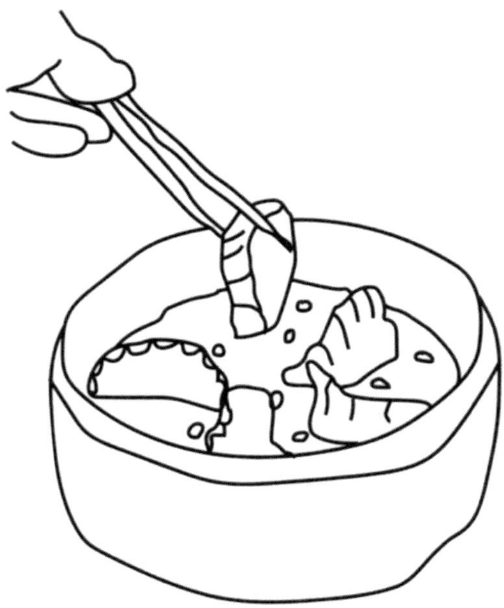

Treat YoSelf

Be kind.
Respect yourself.
Failure is a part of a wealthy life.
Smile.
Laugh often;
It's not a bad life.
Play your strengths.
Be a good friend.
Don't allow distractions.
Don't hold grudges.
Don't be bitter, just be better.
Strive,
Stretch
& grow through life.

I totally got this.

-conversations with myself in the mirror.

Step One: Ask for Help.
Step Two: Allow others to help you.
Step Three: Don't feel bad for letting them help you.

You do not lack the
creativity
ideas
or work ethic;
You lack execution.
Just because you lack
does not mean you cannot gain.
Gain over time.
Learn over growth.
Grow over love.

Ask yourself
what you think you really want to do
in this moment,
right now.
What do you really enjoy doing
and do it.
Don't chase something
and worry about the outcome.
Now,
go chase your sunset.

Living

It is so eye-opening how much peace comes from letting go of the way you thought things should work out, and embracing the FACT that things are working and happening not just to you
but for you.

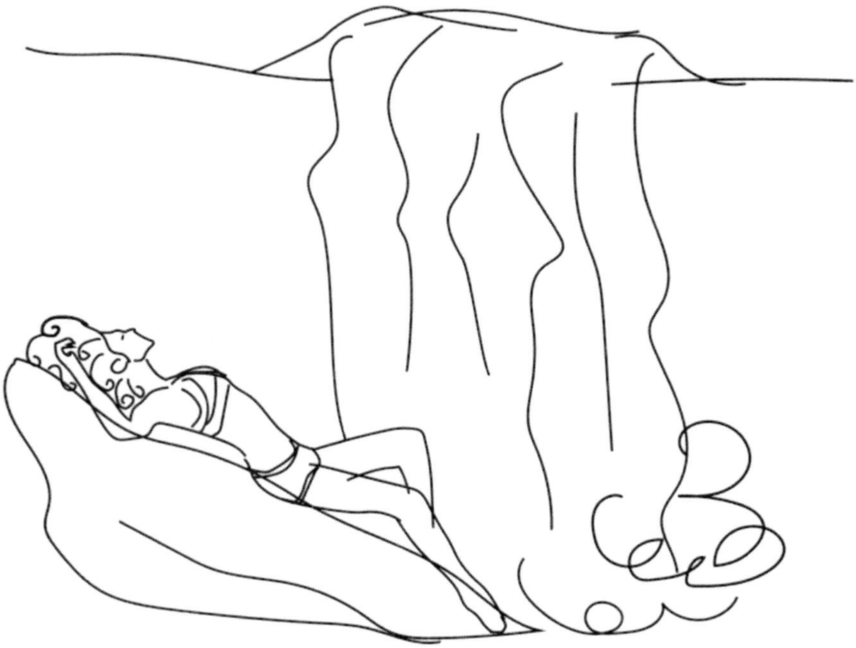

Fitting in is a conspiracy theory.
Pretending to be someone you're not
is a fallacy.
Basing our ideals on someone else's programmed
ideology
of what "success" looks like
is pure insanity.
I'm blessed because
what I thought I wanted years ago,
I didn't get,
& for that,
I am eternally grateful.
Divine Intervention
looks a lot like surrendering into the
Unknown.

Chapter 4
Culture

If you want to master your day,
master your morning.
Self-discipline
is the key to unlocking your full potential.
Make a choice of how you want to start your day
and follow through.
This is a way to create massive momentum.

Dear Black Community,
We are too old and too educated to be unorganized.
Going
Where I am Celebrated,
Where I am the majority.
You are who you surround yourself with.
Therefore,
Kings and Queens,
We are Excellence,
Black Excellence.
We
Are
The Culture.

I pray.
You pray.
We Pray.

We fall.
We break.
We fail,

but then we rise.
We heal.
We overcome.
-something powerful.

Sisterhood

I respect you fully
regardless of your beliefs.
There is space for all of us.
Sisters are Sisters.
Love is Love.
My intention for sharing was to
encourage you to expand &
come back to yourself.

A Seat At The Table

Not as someone's guest.
It gets hard for everyone.
For some,
harder than for others.
Perhaps problems don't stop signs.
But
rather guide lines to a personal path.
Tough times don't last forever;
tough people do,
Being capable of finding humility in the struggle
and in success.
The end goal remains in focus.
Everyday mishaps and obstacles are not up for
distraction.
Found in demeanor.
Do what must be done
in order to survive and get better.
To be able to do it all on your own and without help;
Truly a beautiful skill.

Intentions

Dealing with a desperate person is a two-edged sword;
it's difficult to truly know where the intentions lie.

If you forgive someone for something they did to you,
it doesn't mean you agree with what they did
or believe that
what they did was right.
Forgiving that person means
you have chosen not to dwell on the matter anymore;
you have moved on with your life.

Womban

In Human Design,
I am
a Pure Manifesting Generator for Cave Blending
environments.
Healing my womb naturally
has been a liberating experience.
Many tears & thoughts of
can I do this?
It's a choice
to remind myself that I do not need anything outside of
me.
It's a choice
to sit with the pain of all the women before me.
It's a choice
to sit with the discomfort emerging from silencing my
womb. I love
& choose to forgive her anyway.
She's always been
there.
Always protecting me.
It's my turn to make
that conscious choice
now.
In every moment.

Making a man out of you created a woman out of me.
Radical Responsibility
meets conscious language.
Words are spells,
that's why they call it spelling.
What narratives are we casting?
People use these tactics to protect their hearts.
Ultimately trauma bonding
& then hyping each other up as if it
was some form of Liberation.
This is an invitation to reevaluate the
words we cast on our fellow women.
Sisterhood
to me is about safety
Acceptance &
Respect.
We lead through our embodiment & express through our voices.
Let's honor our sisters
As the Queens
Empress &
Goddess they are.
Discernment is always key.
There's no shame involved here.
In this space, we let it all go & then take Aligned Action.

A Higher Self

All religions are extremely spiritual.
Go to church
and you experience God.
Go pray and you feel the spirit.
You manifest when you pray.
You are praying when you manifest.
Simply believing is
tapping into source.
If there is a higher power of good,
there has to exist of
the complete opposite.
Learning every day
More on this earth plane
What my spirit has signed up for
but I channel in a
divine message to all.
Constantly protect your energy
spirit
physical body
& mental space.
When you feel out of alignment
- pray.

Purging
Releasing
Shame
Guilt
Self-Sabotage
Regret
Unworthiness
I do not move to look a certain way.
I now move to feel a certain way
& my body is a
by-product of the LOVE
I have for myself.
I don't show up
anymore because I
am disciplined.
I show up
because I am devoted
to my vessel
with honor to serve Me.
Everything I put into
my body
is an offering now.
My body is not a dumpster for my emotions
or a slave to my Mind games anymore.
I decided that
before I bless the food I'm about to eat,
I'm blessing my body for being able to absorb
the nourishment.
Grateful for my plate.
Grateful for the hands to hold my plate.
Grateful for the tongue that tastes my food.
Grateful for the awareness to slow down.
It's all creation.
Anyway,
It's all a blessing.
Either way,
No shame;
simply choosing differently than I ever have before.

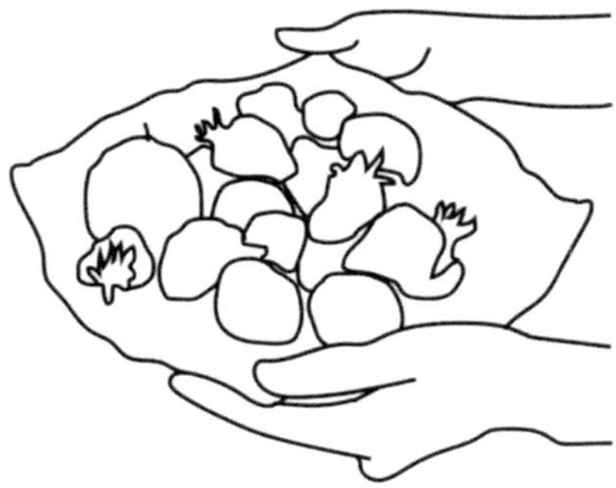

Frequencies speak to me.
Rise up & meet the highest frequency.
Use your perceived challenges as
invitations to ignite your fire.
Let the projections burn as you meet yourself
with Divine Grace.
All I hear is Trust,
Trust,
Trust.
Whether we're conscious of this co-creation or not,
It's happening at all times.
The Universe is conspiring through you
& for you.
This is where Free Will & Divine Will begin to dance
A paradox
because everything is in perfect alignment as it is
and we also have the choice to shift the energy in every
given moment.
Divine Will is always rising.
Will, Free Will.
Choose to do the same.
It's a choice to surrender.
We either create our own current or
get swept up by the currents around us.
I choose to rise above.

Where the Money Resides

Fix your crown.
Drink your water.
Handle your shit.
Keep it pushing.
On your worst days,
remember who the fuck you are.
Now go get this bag.

The Value of Time

Surround yourself with people that reflect who you want to be and how you want to feel; energies are contagious. You can't change the people around you. But you can change who you surround yourself with. You need to associate with people who inspire you, people who challenge you to rise higher. People that make you better. Do not waste your valuable time with people who are not adding to your growth.

Travel often, learn the other cultures, and things will click.

Your destiny is too important.

Spring Equinox

From dark to light.
From seed to fruit.
From water to land.
From abyss to matter.
Feeling grateful.
Feeling humbled.
Feeling expansive.
Feeling powerful.
Experiencing Today's Energy.

The Pandemic

Torn between needing to stay present and connected
so that I know exactly what's going on
& needing to unplug to catch my breath
because I am extremely overwhelmed.

LEACH

As a society,
we were never taught how to live;
only how to operate within the system.
The system doesn't come with a guidebook
on how to care for your human body Self sufficiently
Only with dependency,
cultivating codependency.

Chapter 5
The Lesson through it all

Know Better

You may not understand now.
That's not the lesson.
The lesson is when you do.
Do Better.

Worth

I am no Diamond,
I am much more rare than that;
worth so much more.
I'm sorry it took you so long to see.

Reveal, Remove, Replace

The longer I go without something,
the more comfortable I get with its absence.
Tired of wasting my time on people who treat me good one day,
then act like I don't exist the next day.
Instead of saying "I don't have time",
try saying "you're not a priority".
If it feels uncomfortable,
good.
That's the point.
Changing our language reminds us that time is a choice.
If I don't like how I am spending my time,
I can choose how to spend it differently.

You are only seeing with your internal projection.
People have no idea what is transmitting.
Remember you are prepared for this.
Your emotions will continue to be played
until you realize your safety is an illusion
that you
and only you
can provide for yourself.

The body already knows and is communicating
with you from moment to moment.
The logical mind cannot know more for the body than the body itself.

The heart of compassionate communication
Rooted in love, rooted in compassion.

Conscious partnerships are blissful by nature
because of their deep-rooted commitment to continual
surrender
& grace.
Self-Love doesn't eliminate old patterns
Behaviors
Thought patterns or programs.

With Awareness comes Application.

Let go of the stories,
take responsibility,
surrender
show up
Again
& again
& again.

My Love
journey has
shown me
what it truly
means
to let go of the attachment to the other.

Once you accept that no one owes you a thing, you begin to hold more value in those who go out of their way for you. You are not entitled to a helping hand, a bring-in, or a seat being offered to you. Anything positive you receive from someone is a gift that must be appreciated.

Snip Snip

I used to be so hung up on trying to fix everything and save every relationship, whether it was friends or not. But now, I have realized that life goes on with or without.

-Moral of the story, focus on you and your path. Others will fall in place or get out of the way.

Unfollow people that make you feel bad; very simple,
filter your life
feel joy
chase joy.
It doesn't have to feel bad to be alive.
Life is beautiful.
You owe it to yourself to experience joy love and light.
You deserve good things.
You deserve to smile
every day
to feel peace.
Find that for yourself.
———————————

I am a blessing
I deserve peace
I am my own
peace
I create space
for peace
I am peace
remembering
peace inside me
I am peace
piece by piece, I
release.

Committing yourself to your growth
usually comes with
uncharted territory
which often brings a plethora of emotions.
You were born to feel good &
love your life.
Feeling uncomfortable
A temporary moment
A breakthrough
A mutation.
Every sequential and non-sequential choice plays its part.
Every time we get outside of our comfort zone,
a new timeline & trajectory is created.
Imagine how many quanta leaps you could take just by feeling...
uncomfortable...
Allow your heart to be the highway to your North Star.

Opportunity

The fear of making mistakes
Will keep you in a perpetuated cycle of doubt.
Perfectionism is an illusion dissolved through action.
We can choose to start NOW.
Practice is Improvement.
Practice is Progress.
Be committed to taking seemly "small" steps every day
because they do matter
& it's safe to make mistakes.
Be grateful that you have the opportunity to try again
a true gift.
Feel the fear & do the thing anyway.

Reflection in Stillness

I am still unfolding.
I am still incubating.
I am choosing to water my seeds during this time.
I'm not waiting for a time stamp to begin again.
My body knows where She is & where She is going.
I no longer have to play along with the stories.

I am woman
I am sovereign
I am free to speak my mind
I am woman
I am honored
just to be ALIVE
Asé.

Awaken

It takes forgiving yourself to free yourself.
Dare to dream.
Dare to be unapologetically you.
An unwillingness to forgive quickly turns to anger and well, you know how that goes. Every single version of self that has ever existed
was and is worthy of your forgiveness.
Each one
catapulting you into the next
Again & again.
Give thanks to yourself.
you are here
&
I'm proud of
you.
May these words be a reminder of all that you are and will always be.

SAGE

I was toxic to
some and a
blessing to
others.
I am willing
to admit that
I wasn't
always in the
right.
I am
responsible.
I am
dedicated.
I honor my
vessel.
I honor my
energy in motion.
I am honorable.
I always have a choice.
I choose to respect myself.
Eye am worthy.
Just because I did something wrong in the past
does not mean that I can't advocate against it now.
It doesn't make me a hypocrite.
It shows growth.
It shows I am human.
Don't allow others use the past to invalidate the mindset.
Growth
is a concept,
embrace it.

It's only when you stop, do people realize how much you used to do for them.
If I could change one thing about myself, I would STOP over-giving.
People get comfortable, they find a stray high horse
and they build a house on it.
Entitlement is a disease;
Focus on yourself.

Free yourself from the thoughts of others.
Do not let their traumas project on you.
Hop into your bag of prosperity.
Feed your soul.
Feed your heart.

Hopping around from one relationship to another does not give you time to heal.
You damage those around you with the trauma you have endured.
People vibrate.
People match energies.
Heal yourself first.
Discover your authentic energy.
The time you have wasted moving from one soul to another
can be spent on your own.
Quite frankly,
my time you have wasted is not wanted nor is appreciated.
Heal yourself first.

Ownership

Once you free yourself from the thoughts of others,
you will allow your own light to shine through the cracks.
The universe radiates the conscious thoughts you give it.
So, give it abundant thoughts.
It is you who determines your own destiny.

Eight Rules of Life.

1. Make peace with your past so it won't disturb your future.
2. What other people think of you is none of your business.
3. The only person in charge of your happiness is you.
4. Don't compare your life & circumstances to others: Comparison is the thief of joy.
5. Time heals almost anything. Take some time for yourself.
6. Stop analyzing everything. It's okay to not have all the answers.
7. Smile, your worst days are someone's best days. It could always be a lot worse.
8. Don't take it personal.

Chapter 6
Happy Sunsets

I am not linear; I am a beautiful maze.
My words are from the heart,
my mind is always in a daze.
I want a love that's free,
a love that's not linear.
I want to adventure all the days of my life,
an adventure of a lifetime.
A life well spent,
my life.

Those difficult conversations are worth having.
-moving forward.

I don’t like to pick up and leave at your disposal or expense.
I decide when I want to stay.
I decide when I choose to leave.
I am not your used tissue.

The universe has a funny way of showing you who has your best interest at heart.

Things will work out.

They always do.

25th Solar Return

My heart has never beamed brighter.
This essence of mine is freer than she's even been.
Higher than she's ever soared.
My dreams could never capture the depths of this experience.
Eternal gratitude.
Eternal life.
Growing, still.
Learning, always.
I am surrounding by soul much Love
even amongst my darkest hours!

Understand that it was never you;
you were never the problem.
Some people just needed you in their life for a great lesson.
Sometimes it's hard to understand but give yourself time.

To the love that I thought was my life,
You're not.
I love you anyway because love is my life.
It's so easy to believe in someone's intentions rather than their actions.
Don't get so caught in reading between the lines that you don't read the actual lines.

doing well> meaning well.

Instead, I choose to focus more loving on me.
Every part of my being is worthy of the most exceptional Love.
We are all capable of getting
out of our own way.
We're able
because we're willing.

I’m in bliss with this human.
My days with you remind me this is all but a dream
for everything is an illusion but this.

Your pearls are your gifts.
They deserve to be showcased.
You are safe to express your magic.
When we are not in the state of being sacred,
meaning connected to the source,
to the belief that you are always safe & protected,
we are in the illusion of being -sacred.
Although valid, truth will always rise above illusion.
You are worthy of this reality.
My shell is my home,
not my shield.
In my shell, I am sacred.
In my home, I am sacred.

Accepting Faith

Every day it rained
led me to believe that the sun was nonexistent,
that the God I've been praying to was maybe nonexistent too
like I couldn't be heard
or even seen at one point.
I tried to hold space for fate and trust because I needed to believe
in something greater than myself.
I would say it doesn't hurt me to have faith
but then again, I'd be pretending
like walking away from everything I knew didn't leave me black and blue,
as if the scars of mine don't tell stories about centuries of pain,
like the women in my family before me weren't
forced to not have a voice of their own.
Maybe they too were owned by their own demons.
So today, I free them
from the trauma.
Today, I rewrite my story
not only for me but for all the women before me
and for all the little girls with dreams bigger than their hearts.
It's time for a new start.
It's time we have faith.

———————————————————

leaning into the acceptance of faith,
spreading it across this world like butter.
It's time we have faith that something greater than us is working for us.
May we find the courage to strategize & scrutinize the blueprints our ancestors left for us.

To be unalike
separate
sea parts
see parts
of yourself
in others
reflection in the water
sinking into the darkness of the shadow
to be forgotten
or lost in them
as if we were never them.
Can we remember?
Can we remember the reflection of self
or can we only see
separation?
Hidden in the shadows of reflection
is where we find wholeness.

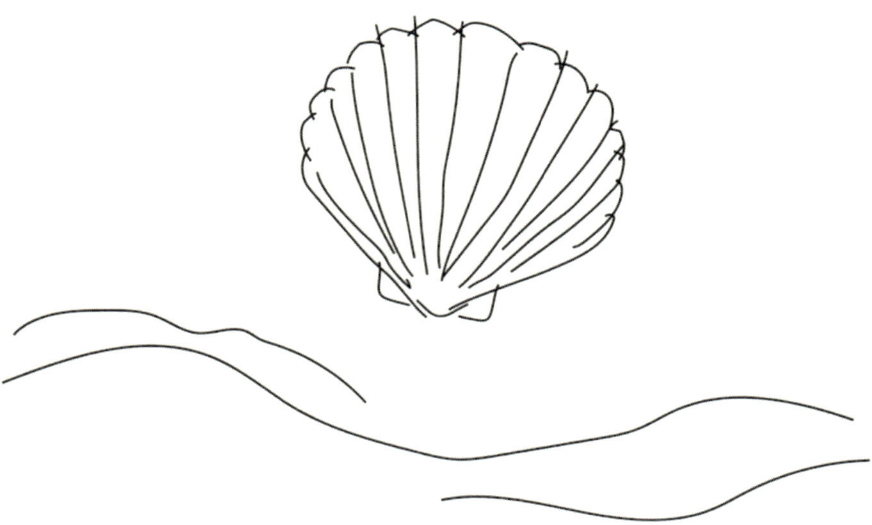

My body is self-healing, and I am already healed.
I remember who I am by letting go of stories I created about myself.
Lost in the illusion of a
dopamine rush from the
validation of others even
though I'm doing this for
me.

Water your own;
Find the green that lies ahead of you and
cling to it so you, the fruit can grow and pollinate this world
with positivity and love.

Existence:

This Month is
going to be a BIG month for you.
Let go of bad energy,
negative thoughts,
and what no longer grows you.
Create space for all you desire.
You have a fresh start ahead of you, so
be ready to grow,
heal
and upgrade
in every area of your life.
Your thoughts manifest your desires.
Introduce powerful,
significant thoughts into your brain's frequency and then
witness your mindset shift & your desires come to life.

She knew no thing
was greater than her own embodiment of Love.
She reminds me that softness and laughter are powerful too
to all the versions of self that have ever existed & will continue to exist
on this earth plane and beyond,
I love you.

Note to self;
may genuine self-expression and grounded communication
find you
in the midst of every reflection mirrored back to you.

Love is Evolution

What's inner stood & overstood doesn't have
to be explained.
I am whole.
He is whole.
I embody respect.
He embodies respect.
Partnership is a dance with Source.
These bodies are vehicles of expression.
Beyond the distortion of their powerful yet subtle
energetic capabilities.
"It takes 2 to tango"
This beautiful human being jumped timelines into
my reality and we've been living ever since.
We're not committed to "forever", we're
devoted to eternal love,
that which is greater than Self.
I want so much more in this life with you.

For all the storms you put me through,
For all the unshakable moments of anxiety,
For all the worst days I have survived,
The times when circumstances challenged my emotions and challenged me to vibrate higher,
I thank you.

Chapter 7
I am still learning

Everything is in divine order.
Your ego is the one having a hard time accepting your reality.
What is to come is greater than your fears.
Stop holding onto anger and negativity and let Spirit and Divine take over.
You are triggered again and again because it's a show and your energetic remembrance is the audience.
We are not victims.
Say it again.
Embody it!
Let go and let God.
A faulty,
imperfect,
jaded,
traumatized human does not know better for the collective of you.
If someone isn't in control of you,
you feel out of control and that's the problem.
Can you even remember your own sovereignty before you met them?
No, because they tell you every day how to live,
how to act,
how to feel.
It's no secret that you are chosen, and this is your life, so, live it.
Take back your life-force energy.
They do not deserve your Inner Energy.
You are powerful beyond human comprehension.
Walk beautifully.
Talk beautifully.
Live beautifully.

A Rich Mind

Observing the observer
grants me the opportunity to pause and respond in the now
and not in the trauma.
We have been coached to live in this cultivation of trauma and be okay with it
when things are not in fact okay.
The trauma stops here.
I am what my ancestors prayed for.
I am the lineage that will stop the trauma culture and build wealth within this generation.
Wealth is health.
Wealth is spirit.
Wealth is being.
And it starts with me.

Allow yourself to receive all the good things coming to you.
Choosing ultimate surrender,
choosing to be present
in the chaos
the stillness
the beautiful and ever-wavering humanness
breathing in what's meant for me,
emptying what doesn't serve purpose,
choosing discernment,
peace in immersing in what is
what can be,
what we choose to be,
where we choose to take ourselves
fully and utterly willing to be
and so it is.

A contributing factor to the hardships that people face include barriers related to;
race, sex, and religion.

Black Lives Matter.
Today.
Tomorrow.
Forever.

Learning is a derivative of curiosity and travel.

Stop having friendship problems with people
who aren't friends
and stop having relationship problems with people
who aren't committed.

"You discover through your losses that life isn't about what you have but about who has you".

Master the little things, and work on them every day.
Create these devotional habits for yourself to practice.
Every day will not be the same,
and every day will not be easy.

You are the epitome of solidarity within you and yourself.
Every time you think you've grown,
BOOM!
more expansion
more expansion
more expansion.
When the going gets tough,
the initiation has begun.

Stay present
because when we worry, we suffer twice.
Some call it mindfulness, others call it being in the zone.
Whatever you call it, you are in this moment,
It can be hard thinking about what is to come,
especially when we feel like there is little we can control.
There will be plenty of opportunities.
Remind yourself that in order to step through these doors,
we have to be ready to receive.
And to be ready means to be present.

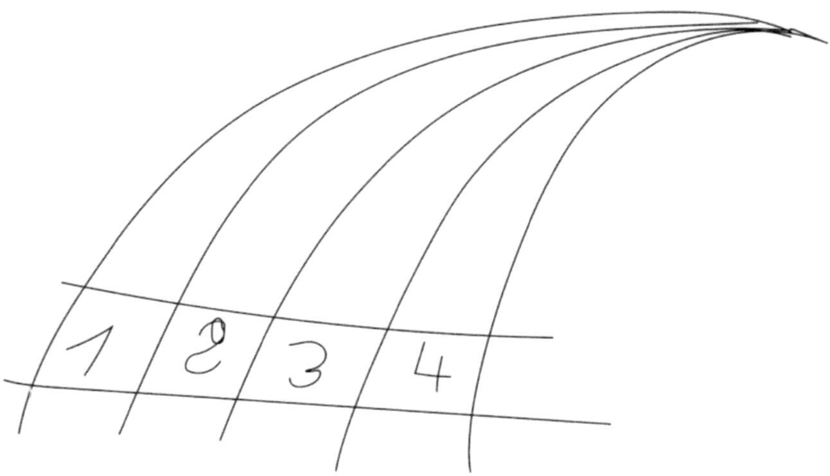

Change is what moves you forward in life.
In order to grow in life,
you must be willing to identify the areas you need to work on
and commit to working on those areas.
Change requires an overwhelming desire to adjust,
sacrifice,
commit
ACTION
& execute.
Keep your eyes on the goal versus the problem at hand!

FORGIVENESS

The liberating action of forgiving is challenging and worthwhile.
When I see my innocence,
I see the innocence within all beings.
When I see myself through shameful eyes,
I place that blanket of shame onto others to wear.
So, I don't feel so alone
ALONE
the zero point of no separation.
It's not a requirement for others to see my reality for me to feel safe.
That is MY choice.
It is up to me to create a safe space
with my own body and honor the life I choose to live without
placing projected judgment onto others
for choosing their reality per their sovereign autonomy.
Forgiveness allows this.
Acceptance allows this.
It's simple, not easy.
I choose anyway.
Tears, frustration & all.

Your divinity is your protection.
It’s easy to forget source created you with wings
when you are offered a parachute.
I trust my intuition.
It is safe to trust myself.
Is it safe to trust others?
I am accepting
I am wise
I am safe
I am
Love dissolves all illusions.

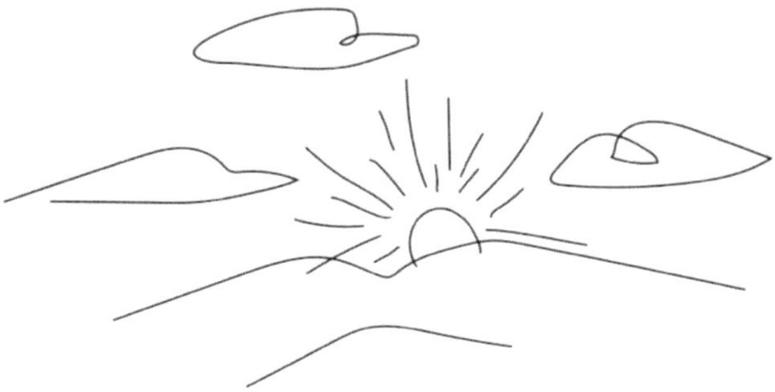

Sweet Rising

I am aware of what no longer serves me.
I am willing to release what no longer serves me.
I am courageous.
I am capable.
I am.
I am the observer of my emotions
and I choose to feel them.
Every beautiful thing you say to someone
becomes a part of them and you.

When the sun comes out,
my mood is elevated to a whole different level.
I am inspired.
I am ushered into abundance.
I am open to receive.
I am honored to be, myself.
I am.
My only limitation is myself.

Release

I release the need to overextend.
I release the need to over-explain.
I release the need to match frequency.
I release the need to leave the now.
I release what no longer serves me.
"My need to do" transforms into my desire to be.

You are not for everyone & that's okay.
The world is full of people
who no matter what you do
will point blank not like you.
But it's also filled with people who will love you fiercely.
You are not for everyone and that's okay.
Talk to the people that hear you.
Don't waste time trying to convince those who don't approve of your value;
you are not for them, and they are not for you.
Politely wave them on and continue your journey.
Sharing your path with someone is a sacred gift;
don't cheapen your gift by facing yours in the wrong direction.
Keep facing your true north because, in the end,
all you have is you.
You are not for everyone and that's okay.

Seek no one's validation but your own.
Small-minded people
will never be able to comprehend your limitless ability.
I choose blessing.
I choose to trust.
I choose to love.
I choose to be.
I choose.
Where there is choice, there is freedom.

Initiating the wild woman within
while creating a container for my masculine to allow her to flow.
It takes two to tangle and life is a dance.
Creation is harmonization.
Only inclusivity exists;
separation is an illusion.
Just as earth is a container for water to flow,
consciousness holds space for sprit to flow.
This knowing has expanded my horizon ten-fold.
Healthy love exists;
remember that.

Perspective

Been saying these simple
words a lot in the last
few weeks. So, here's my
gut feeling like writing it
today;
whenever you're in a
situation that goes left,
practice asking,
"What is this teaching me?" or
when you get triggered
or when you feel your
ego unhealthily takes over,
ask yourself,
"What is this teaching
me"?
It's easy to create the
outlook of a situation of
your day,
but when
everything is a learning
experience and testing
you to overcome lessons,
it's difficult to question
why we experience every
single moment in life.

I am soft.
I am sweet.
I am gentle.
Within my vulnerability
lies strength.
I am.
My tides are powerful,
yet the snowflake is light.
The melting snowflakes find a way back to each other.
We are all a part of something grander.
That's the magic.

My purpose in this life is to drop into
my body & LIVE in my experience.

I am safe in my body.
I am centered and connected.
I am grounded in my roots.
I am open to change.
I am financially secure.
I am.
In this now moment, I know peace.

I am seen.
I am heard.
I am felt.
I am deserving.
I am art.
I am.
The only thing I ever really cared about
was the art.
Finding art inside of everything
makes life a lot more beautiful.
Where there is breath,
there is love.

How do you label that which cannot
be named?
How do you explain that which is undefinable?
In the absence of thought,
freedom emerges.
Everything that touches the skin
EVERYTHING
is absorbed into the blood
consciousness.
Sit with that for a moment.

Love is multidimensional.
There's no playbook for it.
No warning when it's going to rip your heart out of your chest or
when it's going to set it on fire.
Love has no sequence
expiration
or rules.
Love is unconventional and sometimes unexpected.
Never meant to be forced.
Real love
holds you at night and gently kisses your cheeks like the sun in the morning.
Love has no limits or recommended dosage.
Each and every person
has a love language of their own.
Note that your life is never too foreign to understand.
You are never too much.
Live deeply and fearlessly.
Love you.
You deserve that.

Confidence

Self-love.
There is no loving others
without loving yourself.
Others are just a
projection of you.
The world is just a projection
of your inner self.
How do you expect to receive love+ acceptance
if you can't even give it to your own self?
One thing that is helping on this continuous journey of self-love
is knowing my love language & showing it to myself.
I.e., my love language is words of affirmation
& I find it so soothing when I journal
and show gratitude to the
blessings in my life.

Manifestations

Many people don't
know this but the thing
about manifesting is:
we do it all the time.
The choices we make on a
daily basis,
the way we
speak to ourselves as well as others
and the beliefs we
choose to believe are
manifesting our future.
Manifesting your dreams
is only possible when
you match your energy
with the energy of that
manifestation.
So, a bright and cheerful
future filled with
happiness will only be
possible if you manifest
while you are feeling the
elevated emotions such
as gratitude, love, and joy.
Wanting things for ourselves is one thing.
Actually feeling like you deserve to have it is another.
That's why a lot of our manifestations don't come true
because our energy doesn't align with the goal we have.
We say we want to manifest but in reality, we see it as a
dream.
As something unreachable.
Remember: what you want, you already are.
You just need to get on the same vibration as that thing
and that's where changing our limiting beliefs and
shadow work come in.
You are worth your dreams and goals, you just have to
start believing you are.

Roll with the Tides

The tide doesn't question itself as it's pulled back out to sea.
Define the phrase "ebb & flow" ~ a recurrent or rhythmical pattern of coming and going or decline and regrowth.
You see, for a while, I played victim to this saying.
I either didn't honor my "ebbs" or completely milked them to stay complacent.
Not realizing it's simply a word that I give meaning to.
It didn't define me and the stories I attached to ebbing were simply that.
STORIES.
Truthfully, labeling is just another way for the mind to create linearly.
Often forgetting that within that very cycle is rebirth.
An ebb is not the end but the beginning.
In the same way, energy does not die, it simply transforms/transfers.
What if.
Instead of creating a story about why we aren't doing enough, we get honest about where we're at without the labels.
*We ask ourselves how we can meet ourselves with grace and show up fully in this now moment no matter what that looks like.
Going within is the very thing that springs you forward.
Trusting your unique process was the way through.
We didn't label where we are as "good" or "bad" and we honored ourselves in neutrality.
Slow movement was the momentum that brought the wave
back to shore
AFFIRM THIS WITH ME
"FAST OR SLOW, I AM ALWAYS IN FLOW".

I am my own lane.
I am my biggest critic.
I am my biggest supporter.
I am my own competition.
Only surrounding myself with those that bring out the best in me.
My peace is too precious.
Thankful for those that are in my life.
You all add so much value and always make me feel so loved.

Remain in the moment but learn when to drift to your own path.
If you stay too long as a servant leader,
you become a slave.
A slave to someone else's dream
and ability to grow at a height that you far exceeded way before time.

I am surrounded by the vastness that is love.
I am held so tenderly even when my thorns are present.
Love spoke to me about the four elements
[earth, air, fire and water] and said "Earth holds space for water"
Earth isn't necessarily an element itself but a space holder.
Land splits itself to give water a home.
Water parts the ways-navigating organically and without permission.
But what about fire, I asked.
Does that mean Air holds space for fire?
Yes, Fire dances with the wind so poetically,
it has its own rhythm and heartbeat.
Earth and Air hold space for water and fire.
In the same way, being grounded (earth) allows emotions and feelings to flow freely (water) or stepping into intellect and mental intention (air) allows passion, discipline and motivation to cultivate (fire).
A reminder that we are nature experiencing itself, appearing as individuals - just long enough to remember separation is an illusion.
Nature shows us how beautiful death truly is.
Death = transformation

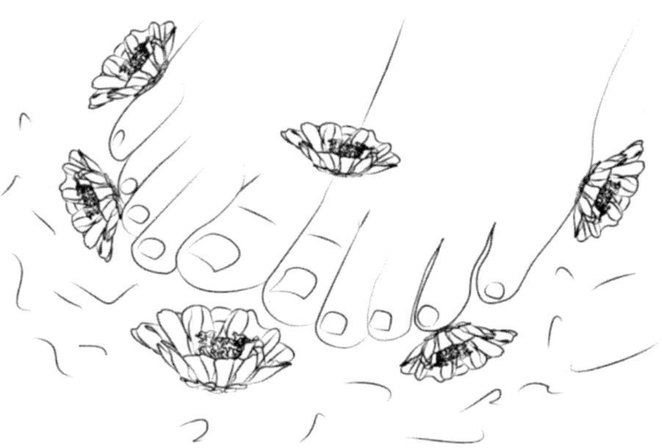

Clear skin is happy skin.
Stress-free skin.
Lots of water skin.
Good company skin.
Healthy boundaries skin.
Self-healing skin.
Personal growth skin.
Choosing joy skin.
Flourishing.
Glowing.
You cannot control anything that is not attached or a part of you.
All waiting is futile; to depend on time to solve our problems is self-delusion.

Promote yourself and your highest level of vibrational frequency.
The light is your energy
and your candle will allow you to vibrate and flow
with the beat of you.

What would my life be like had I never fallen for you?
Would I have a changed sense of what love looks like?
Would I be more in love with the process of loving myself?
Would I be happier?
Would I wonder every time I turn the corner?
Or the next time we might lock eyes and feel uncomfortable dispositions with each other?
Is this what it feels like to love someone so much and you let them go?

Healing

I used to be so angry.
I could never understand what I did for you to just disappear.
For you to be so grown yet so childish.
How could you not articulate your feelings?
How could you not express what was bothering you?

We were so vulnerable with each other,
physically,
mentally,
and spiritually.
But you left me wondering;
What did I do wrong?
What did I miss?
You broke me.
You acted like I didn't exist;
only came around when it was convenient
and left.
Left again shortly after.
Just when I thought I was over you,
you made your way back in.
Shame on me for thinking you changed.
Seeing the best in people can cause a lot of hurt.
How dare you try and come back?
Do you not understand the epitome of your destruction?
All I wanted to do was love you.
I wasn't selfish enough for myself.
I didn't have the strength to let you go.
I acknowledged my feelings for you
and truly understanding that people come and go,
but experiences and lessons stay.
I acknowledged my own feelings
and planted myself so deeply that I was rooted in my
own epitome of self-love.
Having a pure heart and genuine intentions will take you
so far in life.
When you invest into people and add value to their lives,
support,
care
and compassion
will always find you.

The taller the building,
the longer it takes to lay the foundation to handle the growth.
If you're outgrowing who you've been,
you're on the right path.
Keep evolving.
Evolving involves eliminating.
Reclaim your time.
What good is it to keep people or situations around that consistently take up my positive energy to give back and contribute to the world?
When you ask yourself this question and you find the answer,
make the necessary changes.

I am all I have

Entertaining someone who only wants to be entertained.
Losing you, I have myself to gain.
Getting rid of the pain.
Decompressing my brain.
Washing you out.
Getting rid of those stains.
Letting it all work out.
Choosing not to feel this emotional drain.
I guess you were right.
I have changed.
And losing you, I had myself to gain.

Chapter 8
Avocado Thoughts

*If I had a conversation with Life and the Universe, it would go something like this.

Me: I sure could use some help.

Universe: Be careful what you ask for.

Life: But first...

pandemic
global warming
war
plague
systemic issues.

Me: What happens next?

Life;

We don’t deserve dogs

I think my dog laughs in his sleep.
I for sure know he runs and barks.
Does he know he is dreaming?

My place of regroup

Some of the best interviews
pep- talks
sold out concerts
arguments
and more
are pre-arranged in the comfort of my shower.

I often wonder if my confidence rubs off on other people.
I wish it would rub off on me.

#old thoughts

If your friends
don’t help you get to the bag
and keep you from the bag,
those aren’t your friends.

It's okay to be ghetto once in a while.

When you don't feel like getting up in the morning,
Pick a song
Upbeat
Blast it
Dance like there's no tomorrow
And smile.

The best friendships are low maintenance.
Need I say more?

Find someone you can share the other half of your avocado with.

When you come out, it is not the same.
You try your very best to reintegrate back into society.
You try your best to find a job
and a place that will allow you to call home.
You're free.
But are you really free?
You don't even understand the very meaning.
Reintegration;
Now, does that happen before or after
you've gentrified my community?

Grow up and solve your own problems.

Dear math,
There is no equation that will solve for my Y:
Y= my X keeps popping back up

I hope there are days when your coffee tastes like magic,
your playlist makes you dance,
strangers make you smile,
and the night sky touches your soul.
I hope you choose to fall in love with yourself
over and over again.

Sunshine

There is great joy in seeing today and embracing tomorrow.
There is being in you,
there is being in your thoughts and actions.
There is kindness in your spirit;
kindness in your words and heart.
The earth smiles with every flower
and brightens with every moon.
You are the ultimate gift;
sunshine is where you are.

You're supposed to clip the roses, my dear.

Trim the leaves,
cut the ones with no life
so that the nutrients can be absorbed by the whole plant.
Keeping dead leaves blocks the nutrients from the plant.
You are just watering old habits and dead situations.
Stop blocking your blessings.

Don't stop being whole.
Let your light shine.
Some people are so broken,
they get mad at you for being whole.
Surround yourself with people who possess the ability to calm you
with their presence alone.
Everybody must be held accountable.

Rome
was not built in a day.
But also
the first of its kind,
look how beautiful it turned out.

Our Nude bodies are our vessels
in their most vulnerable and raw form.
It's not sexual unless you give it that meaning.
I breathe life into my body.
My body is sacred.
My body is purposeful.
I honor my body.

Once you stop looking, things find you.
Earthside together is where I long to be.

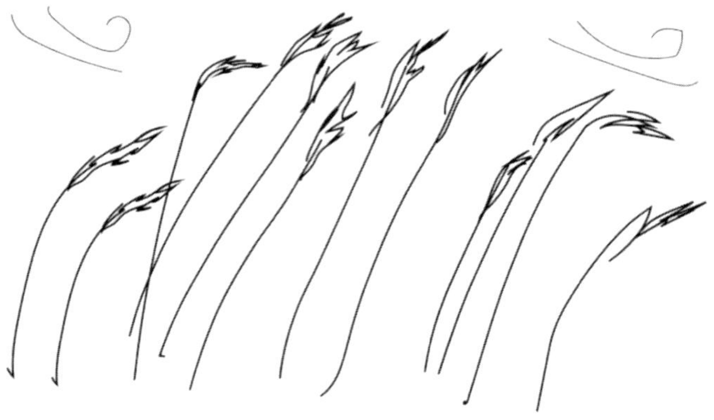

The stillness of her wake sends vibrations
beyond the human ear.
Sunshine pouring onto sunflowers.
I call this the awakening.

Who am I when I just am?

Nothing to do.
Nowhere to be.
Nothing to be.
I am nothing and everything at once.
The epitome of a paradox
like mixed-matched socks.
Was I saying anything at all?
Words only have the meaning we give them,
the power we give them.
Maybe these words hardly hear meaning at all.
In that case, making them nothing
you see.
If it's not the absence of being,
it is entirely based upon the presence of being
simultaneously
aware of the vastness that is you
ever-flowing,
always growing
for there is no time to rush,
no need to rush
because there is nowhere to be.

Lessons Learned, I am still learning

Lessons I've learned;
Pain to Purpose.
Use your gifts to contribute; learn your purpose.
Fill your moments of loneliness with something whole.
You must have the right business partners.
They will walk with you on your path to purpose.
Use the gifts given to you to be a blessing in someone else's life.
You must use them.
As each part does its part,
everything grows.
Do not let your stubbornness block your blessings.
Contribute through your gifts,
through your talents, through your platform, through your education.
Life is about how much you can contribute to someone else.
The most powerful resources at times are the painful experiences we have overcome.
Don't waste your pain,
use it.
Allow your pain to propel you forward
and help those around you in this universe.
Your most effective contributions will come from a place of hurt and sadness
created through life to propel you forward.
Be an uncynical believer.
Use your pain for a purpose.

The more I learn, the more I learn

At the root of it all, we had no foundation.
Cracks that caused concern.
Lack of trust that stagnated us both.
How did you expect us to grow?
Love is not painful.
Growth requires growing pains*.
Growing pains come from obstacles.
Obstacles create friction.
Friction is needed for you to grow.

If your emotions block your vision,
your vision wasn't big enough.
You have the power over your mind,
not outside events.
Realize this and you will find strength.

Thrive in the mess
and don't let people tell you
how to be happy.

Some people may not grow with you because
it's not that important to them.
People may not like you
for the sole reason that
your growth makes them uncomfortable
and upset with themselves.

Not why me, but why not me:

Stop giving the negative so much room to outgrow the positive.
Spend your energy working on the good,
manifest the positive,
and positive things will start to align in your life.
Your energy is what you control.
Vibrate with higher beings.
What you surround yourself with is what you become.
Don't be a chameleon to your environment,
stand out and stand up.
Your inner power emits a higher frequency outwardly that people can feel.
That power you possess within yourself
can scare people if they haven't found it themselves.
But that's when you know
who is authentic
and who is faking it.

Repeat Daily:

I will remain focused on my goals.
Even if I have a moment of difficulty,
I will not give up.
I know success comes with consistency.
I know that I will make it.
Things will get better.
No problem or challenge will stop me.
Everything I deserve is coming my way.

People don't like it when you have more capacity
than they have the container.
Look at your life and see where you are pouring more
into a lesser thing.
We're usually scared to seek something greater than our
own capacity,
but I've learned that people willing to see & risk it,
generally, grow to the level that they're willing to pour.
Quit playing small & safe!
Nothing and nobody owes you less;
you owe yourself more.

#matchcapacity #pourwisely

Food For Thought

Stop being so available and vulnerable
with people who always put you last.
Stop giving do-overs for people who treat you like leftovers.

I lost and found myself within the same sentence.
Detaching from who I once was
to allow myself to cultivate
and embody the essence of love within me.
With intentions only to spread and share it.
Unconditionally,
for my love would be meaningless
if I kept it all to myself.
My grandmother taught me that.

I will continue to show up as my authentic self because I deserve peace
regardless of if others are able to meet me there.
I will always greet myself on the other side
with kindness and respect.

We are constantly being stimulated in a world full of
instant gratification.
We can choose to be present.
We can choose to insource.
We can choose to ground in our truth.
I can't be bought by a dopamine rush.
I am the dopamine rush.
I am the high.
Money can't buy me.
A degree doesn't validate my wisdom.
Sovereign & Free
is the only desire to light my fire.

So many people are focused on what they can gain from any relationship.
Be focused on just being a good person.
The physical fades, but substance lasts.
Looking for somebody solely to have cute babies will have you hurt out here.
Go deeper than the surface.

Match my ambition.
What are your plans,
goals,
and dreams?
Okay,
you make money?
That’s what’s up.
You're fine for real
but what else?

Want to impress me?
Stick around
since nobody else seems to be able to.
Honestly,
Impress me with your:

1. Kindness
2. Integrity
3. Humility
4. Generosity

Quality> Quantity.

Unhappy people ruin stuff,
often unwittingly.
Do not try to change them.
In turn, their unhappiness and frustrations will take a toll on you
and eventually, change your spirit.
Instead, help them get help.
Unhappy people are dangerous.
If you have a choice,
get and keep miserable people out of your life.
Happiness is in,
bitterness/mean-spiritedness is out.
You are too valuable to let the toxicity of others remove you from alignment.

You must start thinking like you're blessed,
talking like you're blessed,
and acting like you're blessed.
That’s how blessings get activated.
A grateful heart is a magnet for blessings.

If you're not careful,
it's easy to get caught up in the things that don't matter
and distracted by things that won't help you reach your
goals.
When you start to depend on social media for a
validation
as to whether you're on track,
it affects your overall attitude and mindset.
Therefore,
take your mental breaks when you can
and do not let your spirit be consumed
by everything that is and is not.

Human beings cannot be saved,
or fixed
or grown by others.
They can only be loved.
So,
love them
and love them well.

When you celebrate the success of others
you experience more success of your own.
And you enjoy life a whole lot more.

When you ask the world to reveal stuff to you,
you better have tough skin
because it's definitely not always what you want to see and hear
and you have to be okay with some things just not being for you.
Even if it's something you really wanted
or thought was for you,
you have to trust what the Universe is showing you and let it go with ease.
It can be hard but
I always find peace in knowing that if the Universe is showing me that something isn't for me,
no matter how many times it happens,
the Universe has something better for me.
I can't see what that is
or when it's coming
but my faith is way too strong not to believe that better days are coming.

Stop chasing people.
If they block you,
cut you off,
or ignore you,
let them go.
Let people naturally come to you and enjoy your energy.
We spend too much time clinging onto people, so they don't leave.
Appreciate those who are there by choice.
Not because you chased them every time they left.

I don’t want to rekindle an old friendship unless the
Universe tells me to.
The Universe has removed them for a reason
and the only new friendships I desire are the ordained
ones.
Unhealthy friendships
hold just as much weight as
unhealthy relationships.

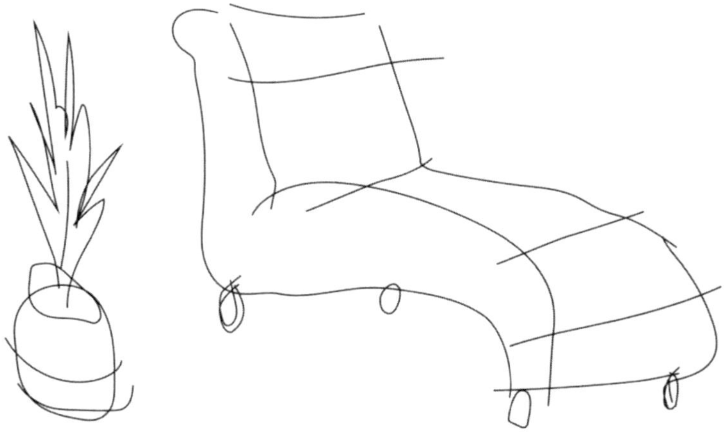

Through meaningless sex,
unattached relationships
and using desire to validate your ego
makes it easy to pretend “I’m not hurt”
Distractions.
Temporary pleasure won’t heal you.
Temporary company will not fill the void within you.
We all have work to do and healing to attend to.
A strong being takes the time to heal
rather than attending to distractions.
Healing is hard to do
but it’s worth it.

March 8, 2018

All it takes is one sip.
Drunk in love.
Drunk in lust.
No alcohol.
Just drunk off touch.
She's a full-bodied colorant;
So velvety yet so bold.

I love being loved.
Constantly nurturing the people
and the soil around me
so that when the sun shines on us,
we all grow.
Can't just be anywhere.
Has to be where value is valued
and time is respected.

I will no longer be taking credit
or putting myself on a pedestal for being the influence of others' "copy".
I am merely a catalyst for activating their true selves
regardless if their intentions are pure or not.
I am not threatened nor am I angry.
Instead, I feel honored.
If I allow myself to embody hate energy towards
someone who "copies" me,
the only person I am hurting is me.
So today, I relate it all.
I don't own anything in this life except for myself.
So thank you for reminding me
that I am love and light.
Whether it is intentionally spread or not,
I will continue to give.
First to myself, then to others.

Discerning between being observant
and being judgmental.
People who truly care about you
are going to push you to be the best you can be.
Physically and mentally.
Don't have people around who are fine with being average.
Every day, I am given the opportunity to show up authentically or to sleepwalk-
tested to see if I will fall for who I am not
or be able to walk my talk.

Courage

The irony is
that you seek sexual validation in an attempt to fill your emotional void,
yet your fear of real intimacy is what truly scares you.
Fear of vulnerability.
Fear of being seen for who you really are.
You are a facade selfishly hiding behind the available.
A cowardly dog.

Do not mock a pain that you have not experienced.
Our Capacity to love is rooted in our ability
to surrender to vulnerability & transparency,
much like the free spirit of a child.
Nothing to hide, nothing to be
but authentically you.
The true nature of who you are.
Love.

Authenticity is real love.
Soul love.
Makes you feel so good you want to dance love
stories we hold onto about who we are,
and what we've been through
confine you to a perpetuating narrative of suffering.
I have experienced emotional neglect,
abandonment,
heartbreak,
disappointment,
verbal/emotional abuse,
sorrow,
self-pity,
anxiousness,
depressive thoughts,
weight gain/loss,
fuck ups,
all while pointing the blame outward

living in a state of victimhood.
I have also experienced immense amounts of joy,
laughter,
happiness,
peace,
abundance,
triumph,
support,
strength,
good health,
and lots of authentic Love.
We must first accept and forgive ourselves
before we can truly transcend
and release the stories that hold us back from radical love
and the life we wish to experience.

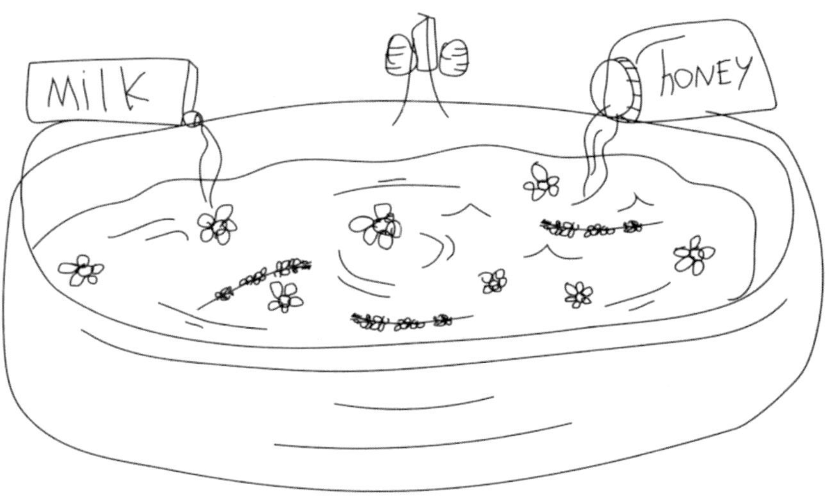

Grateful for this healing.
Grateful to be supported and guided by those who choose self-awareness.
Grateful to be seen clearly.
Grateful for this overflow of love.
Where you find comfort outside of yourself will soon become a reflection
of that which you neglect to give to yourself.
The devil is in the details.
Take a closer look, see more.
This is what magic feels like.

If time is an illusion
as created by men, then you are never short on time,
for it does not exist.
In the same token we use to measure growth,
what if we choose to skip the in between
and allow ourselves to fully embody the knowledge
that we already have by deciding that we are here now.
creating acceptance,
silencing the ego
and remembering that we never forgot anything?
There is no time gap between who, what, and where you
want to be and where you are at now. We create the
illusion of a time gap.
The time gap only exists when fear exists.
Fear is cultivated by experience,
created by the mind.
So, what happens when you decide that fear does not
exist?
The time gap no longer exists.
Meaning, it's all here.
Right now,
If we decide that.
The idea of perfection
creates an illusion that can never be attained without
creating a false identity
or reality.
Grateful to be messily authentic whilst submerged in all
of earth's beauty.

Learn the difference.

It takes a lot of patience,
strategy,
and selflessness
to be with someone like you.
Some talk to you in their free time, and some free their time to talk to you.

Not here nor there.
Above it all.
Between every crack.
In the midst of a dance with chaos,
I'm moving
Evolving ever so gracefully
Like every move was done tactically,
Purposefully,
Inevitably.
I am everywhere.
I am everything,
because everything is
Everything.

02.02.22

When you're in alignment with your authentic self,
the right people will gravitate towards you.
Consolidation is key.
Part of this life
is knowing that you will trigger people
and know it will have nothing to do with you.
The key is to remember it has nothing to do with you.
Sometimes being alone is the upgrade.

3.16.2019

The idea that partners have one life together
doesn't resonate with me, not even in the slightest.
We share our experiences together,
yet in the same moment, my partner has their own experiences
and so do I.
We are all humans experiencing "life"
which allows us to share experiences with one another.
Perception,
trauma,
childhood.
Personal interactions
and environments
alter each individual's experiences
and frankly, it would be selfish of me to say we are sharing a life.
My partner's space and experience are just as important as my own.
Being able to say I share an experience with another
while allowing them freedom & choice will always
resonate deeply with me.

Only reciprocate the energy and effort you are given.
Never give anyone an ounce more of yourself than they are willing to give you.
It's okay to be selfish sometimes.
Your happiness comes first.
A hard pill to swallow is
people's effort towards you is a direct reflection of where they place you in their life.

I always say
"I'm listening"
when my guides,
the Universe,
Source,
& God speaks to me.
I had the realization that all along,
I've been following the very seeds I planted for myself.
Every synchronicity was left with intention.
Reminding me daily of the beauty of life.
If I choose to see it.
If I choose to remain open.

A Sweeter Love

Set apart
Confidently
unalike
A body of art
So obscure
But she
is the cure.
Allure is in
every way
A drug you
need every day
A symbol of
hope
A body of light
The very thing
that keeps you
alive.
She is it
She holds
magic in her
soul
For if you let
her go,
You may never
know.

I have a very strong understanding of who I am
and what I want to do with my time here on this earth.
Sometimes I can be thrown off balance,
depending on what's going on in my life
but I always take myself back to "my why".

Dressed well to address well.
I've known less,
playing games
like I was homeless.
Running laps,
Circling my way back to myself
like a relapse
time and time again
because I chose not to see that.
It could all be so simple.
Trying to change my energy with crystals
It's official,
pushed to the edge
about to blow like a whistle
into everything I put myself
into. Growing into every inch of new territory,
a butterfly in all her glory

Miriam Duen

In the midst of chaos,
I choose to surrender.
To the unknown.
To the possibility of miracles.
I release control to create peace.
I am whole.
I am seen.
I am a body of light.
As within,
so without.

Connected
Protected
Unrested
Toxicity affected
grieving to healing
from all the things
mirroring
believing
breathing
needing like I'm not
needy
uneasy
unsettling
questioning
certainty in my
indecision to choose
faith it in
guided by love
remembered authentically
growing into the best of me.

It's not talking of love,
but living in love that is everything.
You cannot be transparent without being vulnerable.

How you treat yourself after you've made a mistake is the real work.
Focus
Meditate
Stay low-key
Grow spiritually
And give yourself grace.

There is no past.
There is no future;
only the present moment exists.
It’s not the emotional attachment
we create that is tied to our memories.
If we no longer have an emotional response from our memories,
liberation is birthed.
To experience emotions
is a gift of the human experience.
Feel Them.
Nostalgia is an energetic remembrance, not emotional.
All you have to do is want it and then let yourself have it.

How can you fear your next chapter when you are the author?
You are in control of what happens next and only your fault to blame
at the smallest details and beginning stages of your decision-making.
Is your heart and motive in the right place prior to decision-making?
Does the impact of your decision reflect well on your loved ones and the next chapter?
What actions help depict you as the person you know you are?

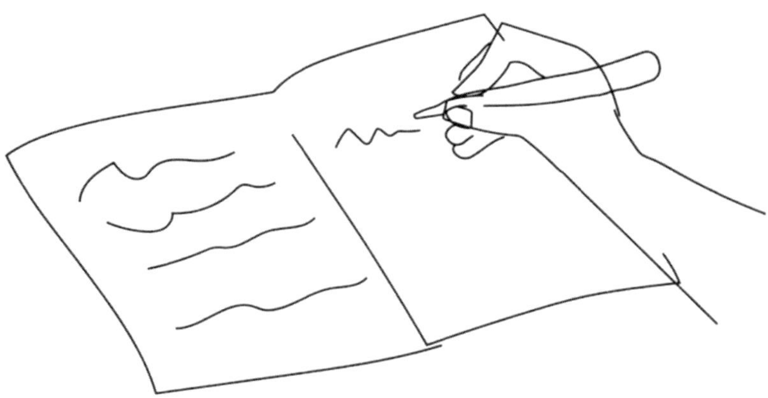

The resistance you feel is proof that you're moving forward.
Grow past it,
stronger and better for having met it.
Doubting your excellence allows for mediocrity to thrive.
Too many people are undermining their value,
whilst others continue to create
without consideration.
Yes, we reside in a world that celebrates surface-level expression,
but the thirst for something real will always
remain supreme.

My intuition cannot be outwitted,
Nor will I be the one to validate your ego.
I am not the threat,
Your insecurities are the threat
But I will happily be the catalyst for your growth,
Wake up.

With Honest Love:

I have reached a zero
tolerance place in my life and
unapologetically have zero space for liars,
projectors
or those who choose self-inflicted pain.
My energy is priceless.
My word is priceless.
It's up to you if you honor yourself in the same way.
I am not employed to take on someone else's life
debilitating morals and values that seem to not exist.
I sit in gratitude for this clarity & knowledge.
I can only pray you chose to align and silence your ego.
The human in you can either destroy you or humble you,
choose wisely.

I am trying to stress to you that the bad days are not permanent
When everything begins to fall back into place,
that's life's way of reassuring you.
The sun always appears
to ensure
that darkness does not overstay its welcome

Clarity rarely comes when the mind is busy, it comes
when the mind is still.
We either spend the same amount of energy
making our lives miserable or making ourselves strong.
My soul is desperately calling for a new environment.

I just want to be
heard
felt
and understood.
Everything else is just noise.
Love is truly the only thing that matters.
Love is the only law
and everything is unfolding divinely.
My love language does not involve affirmation,
but not so much affirmation of my looks or your feelings for me.
Yes, affirm that,
but I mostly crave someone who can affirm my individuality,
my work,
my ambition,
my creativity,
my drive.
I want to be seen fully.

We only meet people that are aligned with us.
How we treat ourselves,
our thoughts,
behaviors.
So if you ever wonder
why you keep meeting the wrong person,
then maybe do some internal work and
see what about you keeps attracting the “wrong” friends/
partners.
It is healthy to have people around you that inspire and
challenge your perspective.
There is no growth in consistent comfortability.

Lack of self-love
is a poison that skews
the lease of reality.
Been lost in the sauce
long enough to know
that
I will never go back.
Nothing can change unless you do.

To the unfolding
The uncertainty that lies behind the unknown
Faith in the divine alignment to and from the universe
Circling my way back to myself
Map on my back
Guided to authenticity
Traveling through the experiences of the world
Feeling everything twice as strong then doubting it
Harmonizing myself to the flow of what is
What will be
What always has been'
Anchoring myself to this feeling
The way my body sings to forty-degree sunrises
Shifting perspective like I am undecided-indecisive
Learning to outlive old versions of myself
Playing roles to play my part
Evolving
A shift in becoming a testatrix
A glitch in the matrix.

Miriam Duen

Hitting Home;

As we go up in levels of leadership, we begin to develop more
responsibilities and more pressure,
problems,
adversity,
More everything.
When you say: “I can’t take this”,
“I can’t handle this”,
“It's driving me crazy”,
You're saying I don’t want to go higher.
You are rejecting the call to moving forward and moving up because
it means more problems.
The problems you deal with right now may be the fact that you are in
training for the next level of leadership.
Purpose does not always feel good.
You have to push through.
You are already here.

I like reassurance
I like attention
I love affection
It's that simple.

Know your worth.
Don't let jaded,
unmotivated
or classless individuals
stop you from grinding
and surpassing the goals you set for yourself.
You did not work this hard to
stay where you are.
Boss up.

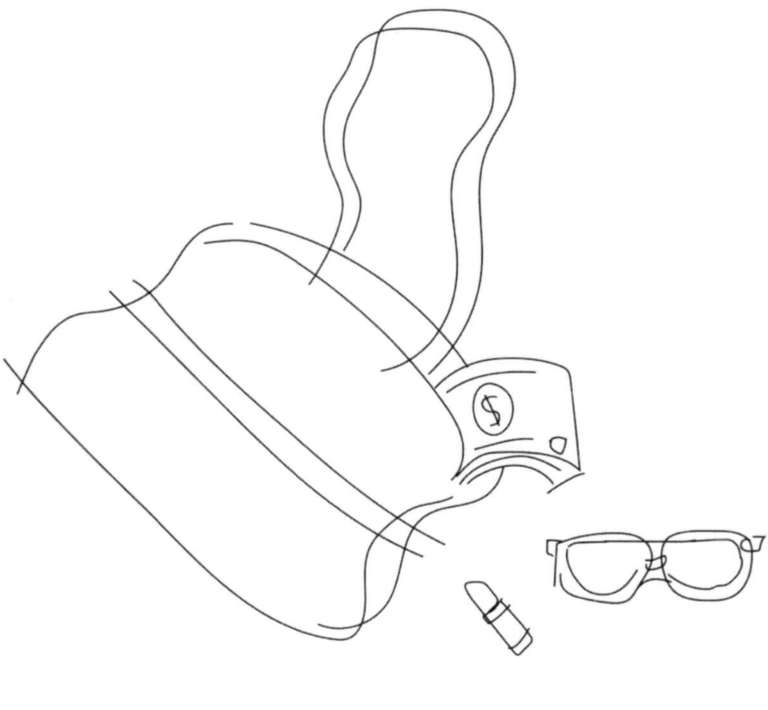

I’m awake,
equally terrifying as it is beautiful.
Every move fluid.
Each vibration felt at an
accelerating rate.
Quick to hold love,
even quicker to feel pain,
remembering,
forgetting,
only to remember
nothing was ever forgotten,
only put away for another day.
At a timed place where I'd need to know
How awake I am,
How easy it is to fall asleep.
These days, I’m an insomniac
dreaming with eyes wide open.
I’m awake.

I love because it’s my natural state of being.
It’s not an emotion or a feeling,
it's my very existence,
it’s what I am.
I give love naturally,
and I’m open to receiving it naturally.
By chance, if it's not reciprocated,
it's no love lost
because I already embody love.

I am protected and guided with each breath.
I have everything I need within me
when I am fearful.
I love myself.
I trust and love myself
for there is nothing to fear.
If this were only for me,
it would be nothing at all.
I am important.
I am purposeful.
I must see that in you
for you to see that in me.

The ART of TRUST:

Fear is cultivated in the mind,
then taken on by the body.
Where the mind goes, the body follows.
Fear is an illusion.
I choose to replace fear with faith.
May worry or uncertainty become present,
I choose to trust

Don't block your blessings trying to do people how they do you.

What you don't cherish, you'll end up losing or sharing. Neglect wisely.

Words from my inner child to yours.
It's safe to play,
to create.
It's safe to feel joy without shame or guilt.
It's safe to rediscover your authenticity.
It's safe to open your heart to love.
My desire is to authentically share my love,
For it would be meaningless if I kept it all to myself.